EONARD
MENTAL
ALONG

CLASSICAL SOLOS FOR TROMBONE

VOLUME 2

TITLE	PAGE	FULL PERFORMANCE TRACK	ACCOMPANIMENT ONLY TRACK
Largo (from *Xerxes*)	2	1	16
Songs My Mother Taught Me (from *Gypsy Songs*)	3	2	17
Minuet No. 2 (from *Notebook from Anna Magdalena Bach*)	4	3	[illegible]
La Cinquantaine (from *Two Pieces for Cello and Piano*)	5	4	[illegible]
See, the Conquering Hero Comes (from *Judas Maccabeus*)	6	5	20
Sonatina (Op. 36, No. 1)	7	6	21
Serenata (from *String Quartet, Op. 3, No. 5*)	8	7	22
Tambourin (from *Second Suite in E Minor*)	9	8	23
Waltz (from *Album for the Young*)	10	9	24
Sonatina (from *Six Pieces, Op. 3*)	11	10	25
Gavotte (from *Paride ed Elena*)	12	11	26
Sonata (Op. 118, No. 1)	13	12	27
Serenade (from *Schwanengesang, D. 957*)	14	13	28
Sonatina (Anh. 5, No. 1)	15	14	29
Bourrée (from *Flute Sonata, HWV 363b*)	16	15	30
B♭ Tuning Notes			31

The enclosed audio CD is also a CD-ROM and includes:
Piano accompaniment for each solo in PDF format for printing.
Tempo Adjustment Software for use with most PC or Mac computers. Instructions included.

ISBN 978-1-4803-5123-3

HAL•LEONARD® CORPORATION
7777 W. Bluemound Rd. P.O. Box 13819 Milwaukee, WI 53213

Visit Hal Leonard Online at
www.halleonard.com

LARGO
from *Xerxes*

TROMBONE

GEORGE FRIDERIC HANDEL
Arranged by PHILIP SPARKE

SONGS MY MOTHER TAUGHT ME

from *Gypsy Songs*

TROMBONE

ANTONÍN DVORÁK
Arranged by PHILIP SPARKE

MINUET NO. 2
from *Notebook for Anna Magdalena Bach*

TROMBONE

Attributed to CHRISTIAN PEZOLD
Arranged by PHILIP SPARKE

00121145

LA CINQUANTAINE

from *Two Pieces for Cello and Piano*

TROMBONE

JEAN GABRIEL-MARIE
Arranged by PHILIP SPARKE

00121145

SEE, THE CONQUERING HERO COMES

from *Judas Maccabeus*

TROMBONE

GEORGE FRIDERIC HANDEL
Arranged by PHILIP SPARKE

00121145

SONATINA
Op. 36, No. 1

MUZIO CLEMENTI
Arranged by PHILIP SPARKE

TROMBONE

SERENATA

from *String Quartet, Op. 3, No. 5*

TROMBONE

FRANZ JOSEPH HAYDN
Arranged by PHILIP SPARKE

00121145

TAMBOURIN
from *Second Suite in E Minor*

TROMBONE

JEAN-PHILIPPE RAMEAU
Arranged by PHILIP SPARKE

00121145

WALTZ
from *Album for the Young*

TROMBONE

PYOTR ILYICH TCHAIKOVSKY
Arranged by PHILIP SPARKE

SONATINA
from *Six Pieces, Op. 3*

TROMBONE

CARL MARIA VON WEBER
Arranged by PHILIP SPARKE

GAVOTTE
from *Paride ed Elena*

TROMBONE

CHRISTOPH GLUCK/arr. JOHANNES BRAHMS
Arranged by PHILIP SPARKE

Grazioso (𝅗𝅥 = 72)

SONATA
Op. 118, No. 1

TROMBONE

ROBERT SCHUMANN
Arranged by PHILIP SPARKE

00121145

SERENADE

from *Schwanengesang, D.957*

TROMBONE

FRANZ SCHUBERT
Arranged by PHILIP SPARKE

SONATINA
Anh. 5, No. 1

LUDWIG VAN BEETHOVEN
Arranged by PHILIP SPARKE

TROMBONE

BOURRÉE
from *Flute Sonata, HWV 363b*

TROMBONE

GEORGE FRIDERIC HANDEL
Arranged by PHILIP SPARKE